Over the Wall

The Story of Paul's Escape in a Basket

We are grateful to the following team of authors for their contributions to *God Loves Me*, a Bible story program for young children. This Bible story, one of a series of fifty-two, was written by Patricia L. Nederveld, managing editor for CRC Publications. Suggestions for using this book were developed by Sherry Ten Clay, training coordinator for CRC Publications and freelance author from Albuquerque, New Mexico. Yvonne Van Ee, an early childhood educator, served as project consultant and wrote *God Loves Me*, the program guide that accompanies this series of Bible storybooks.

Nederveld has served as a consultant to Title I early childhood programs in Colorado. She has extensive experience as a writer, teacher, and consultant for federally funded preschool, kindergarten, and early childhood programs in Colorado, Texas, Michigan, Florida, Missouri, and Washington, using the *High/Scope* Education Research Foundation curriculum. In addition to writing the *Bible Footprints* church curriculum for four- and five-year-olds, Nederveld edited the revised *Threes* curriculum and the first edition of preschool through second grade materials for the *LiFE* curriculum, all published by CRC Publications.

Ten Clay taught preschool for ten years in public schools in California, Missouri, and North Carolina and served as a Title IV preschool teacher consultant in Kansas City. For over twenty-five years she has served as a church preschool leader and also as a MOPS (Mothers of Preschoolers) volunteer. Ten Clay is coauthor of the preschool-kindergarten materials of the *LiFE* curriculum published by CRC Publications.

Van Ee is a professor and early childhood program advisor in the Education Department at Calvin College, Grand Rapids, Michigan. She has served as curriculum author and consultant for Christian Schools International and wrote the original *Story Hour* organization manual and curriculum materials for fours and fives.

Photo on page 5: Penny Gentieu/Tony Stone Images; photo on page 20: Loren Santow/Tony Stone Images.

Library of Congress Cataloging-in-Publication Data

Nederveld, Patricia L., 1944-
    Over the wall: the story of Paul's escape in a basket/Patricia L. Nederveld.
      p. cm. — (God loves me; bk. 49)
    Summary: A simple retelling of the story of how Paul escaped
from his enemies in Jerusalem in an unusual way. Includes follow-up
activities.
    ISBN 1-56212-318-1
    1. Paul, the Apostle, Saint—Juvenile literature. 2. Bible
stories, English—N.T. Acts. [1. Paul, the Apostle, Saint.
2. Bible stories—N.T.] I. Title. II. Series: Nederveld, Patricia L., 1944-
God loves me; bk. 49.
BS2506.5.N45 1998
226.6'09505—dc21
                                       98-15638
                                         CIP
                                         AC

10 9 8 7 6 5 4 3 2 1

Over the Wall
The Story of Paul's Escape in a Basket

PATRICIA L. NEDERVELD

ILLUSTRATIONS BY PAUL STOUB

CRC Publications
Grand Rapids, Michigan

This is a story
from God's
book, the Bible.

It's for say name(s) of
your child(ren).
It's for me too!

Acts 9:20-25

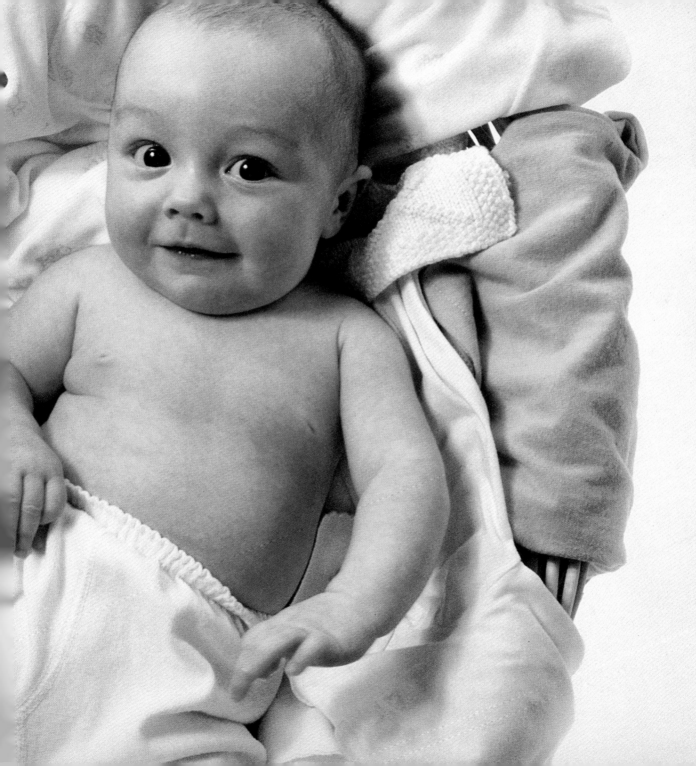

"My friends, listen to me! I want to tell you about Jesus," said Paul. Everywhere he went, people stopped to listen to Paul's good news.

And many people learned to love Jesus.

But not everybody! Some people became angry when Paul talked about Jesus. They wanted to put Paul in jail.

"Hurry, Paul!" said his friends. "Run away from this city before they catch you!"

But it was too late. The angry men were already waiting for Paul by the gate. And a tall wall went all around the city. There was no way for Paul to escape.

Just then Paul's friends had a great idea! "Hurry, Paul. Let's go!" they whispered.

Can you imagine what they're planning to do?

Paul's friends pulled the basket to the top of the city wall. "Hop in, Paul!" they whispered. Then slowly, slowly, slowly they let Paul down the wall.

Paul jumped out of the basket, waved goodbye to his friends, and ran away from the city. He didn't stop until he was far away.

And Paul *never* stopped telling people about Jesus!

I wonder if you love to listen to someone tell you about Jesus . . .

Dear Jesus, thank you for loving us so much. Help us to love you like Paul did. Amen.

Suggestions for Follow-up

Opening

As you welcome your little ones today, greet each one with a soft hug or gentle touch, and tell them that Jesus loves them. Invite them to join you as you form a chain around the room and say, "Hurray! Hurray!"

Gather together in a group and thank Jesus for loving each of you. Sing "Jesus Loves Me" (Songs Section, *God Loves Me* program guide) and other favorite songs.

Learning Through Play

Learning through play is the best way! The following activity suggestions are meant to help you provide props and experiences that will invite the children to play their way into the Scripture story and its simple truth. Try to provide plenty of time for the children to choose their own activities and to play individually. Use group activities sparingly—little ones learn most comfortably with a minimum of structure.

1. Place two or three plastic laundry baskets in your play area. Invite your little ones to climb into them, and remind them of Paul's ride in a basket. Wonder how a grown-up man like Paul could fit in a basket! Talk about the friends who helped Paul, and imagine what it was like to ride down the side of a wall in a basket. God took care of Paul!

2. Invite your little ones to make paper megaphones. Using bright colored cardstock, make copies of the megaphone (see Pattern V, Patterns Section, *God Loves Me* program guide). Or roll your own from a sheet of construction paper. You could also use tubes from paper towels or toilet tissue or a paper cup with the bottom removed. Show your children how to hold the megaphone to their lips and say to each other, "Jesus loves you!" Remind them that Paul told people about Jesus.

3. Make hiding places in your room today. A folding table or two chairs with a blanket stretched over them or large boxes would all make fine hiding places. Your younger children will appreciate open sides and still enjoy playing peek-a-boo. Older children will enjoyed enclosed spaces and a flashlight or two. As they hide, remind your little ones that God keeps us safe, just as he kept Paul safe.

4. Invite your little ones to retell the story of Paul's escape with puppets. Copy the figure of Paul and the basket as directed (see Pattern W, Patterns Section, *God Loves Me* program guide). Let children scribble color the puppet. Or use wooden (non-spring type) clothespins for the puppet and a paper cup for the basket. Loop yarn around the lip of the cup to form the ropes. Create a sense of urgency as children hurry to put Paul in the basket. Then slowly, slowly, slowly let him down. And quickly have Paul get out and tell about Jesus.

5. Tell Paul's story with the song "Jesus Is a Friend of Mine" (Songs Section, *God Loves Me* program guide) as children mimic your actions:

Jesus is a friend of mine.
Praise him. (clap, clap)
Jesus is a friend of mine.
Praise him. (clap, clap)
Praise him. (clap, clap)
Praise him. (clap, clap)
Jesus is a friend of mine.
Praise him. (clap, clap)

Consider using rhythm instruments, bells, or party horns or substituting other actions for the clapping. You may want to add this stanza:

Jesus loves me, keeps me safe.
Praise him . . .

6. Station an adult at each end of a jumping rope and have your little ones hold on with one hand. Take a walk through your building as you sing "Jesus Loves Me." Praise your little ones for telling others about Jesus like Paul did.

Closing

When it's time to say goodbye, gather your little ones together. Whisper "Jesus loves you" into each child's ear, and invite your little one to pass it on to the next child. Or you may just want to whisper it together. Try using different voice levels, inviting your children to mimic you after each one. Thank Jesus for loving each one!

At Home

Remind your little one this week that Jesus loves each of you very much. You might want to pray for friends and neighbors who need to know that Jesus loves them too. Think of ways to tell others that Jesus loves them and that you do too. You might want to bake and deliver cookies, draw a picture, or send a card. As you and your child work together, remind each other of Jesus' love.

Old Testament Stories

Blue and Green and Purple Too! *The Story of God's Colorful World*

It's a Noisy Place! *The Story of the First Creatures*

Adam and Eve *The Story of the First Man and Woman*

Take Good Care of My World! *The Story of Adam and Eve in the Garden*

A Very Sad Day *The Story of Adam and Eve's Disobedience*

A Rainy, Rainy Day *The Story of Noah*

Count the Stars! *The Story of God's Promise to Abraham and Sarah*

A Girl Named Rebekah *The Story of God's Answer to Abraham*

Two Coats for Joseph *The Story of Young Joseph*

Plenty to Eat *The Story of Joseph and His Brothers*

Safe in a Basket *The Story of Baby Moses*

I'll Do It! *The Story of Moses and the Burning Bush*

Safe at Last! *The Story of Moses and the Red Sea*

What Is It? *The Story of Manna in the Desert*

A Tall Wall *The Story of Jericho*

A Baby for Hannah *The Story of an Answered Prayer*

Samuel! Samuel! *The Story of God's Call to Samuel*

Lions and Bears! *The Story of David the Shepherd Boy*

David and the Giant *The Story of David and Goliath*

A Little Jar of Oil *The Story of Elisha and the Widow*

One, Two, Three, Four, Five, Six, Seven! *The Story of Elisha and Naaman*

A Big Fish Story *The Story of Jonah*

Lions, Lions! *The Story of Daniel*

New Testament Stories

Jesus Is Born! *The Story of Christmas*

Good News! *The Story of the Shepherds*

An Amazing Star! *The Story of the Wise Men*

Waiting, Waiting, Waiting! *The Story of Simeon and Anna*

Who Is This Child? *The Story of Jesus in the Temple*

Follow Me! *The Story of Jesus and His Twelve Helpers*

The Greatest Gift *The Story of Jesus and the Woman at the Well*

A Father's Wish *The Story of Jesus and a Little Boy*

Just Believe! *The Story of Jesus and a Little Girl*

Get Up and Walk! *The Story of Jesus and a Man Who Couldn't Walk*

A Little Lunch *The Story of Jesus and a Hungry Crowd*

A Scary Storm *The Story of Jesus and a Stormy Sea*

Thank You, Jesus! *The Story of Jesus and One Thankful Man*

A Wonderful Sight! *The Story of Jesus and a Man Who Couldn't See*

A Better Thing to Do *The Story of Jesus and Mary and Martha*

A Lost Lamb *The Story of the Good Shepherd*

Come to Me! *The Story of Jesus and the Children*

Have a Great Day! *The Story of Jesus and Zacchaeus*

I Love You, Jesus! *The Story of Mary's Gift to Jesus*

Hosanna! *The Story of Palm Sunday*

The Best Day Ever! *The Story of Easter*

Goodbye—for Now *The Story of Jesus' Return to Heaven*

A Prayer for Peter *The Story of Peter in Prison*

Sad Day, Happy Day! *The Story of Peter and Dorcas*

A New Friend *The Story of Paul's Conversion*

Over the Wall *The Story of Paul's Escape in a Basket*

A Song in the Night *The Story of Paul and Silas in Prison*

A Ride in the Night *The Story of Paul's Escape on Horseback*

The Shipwreck *The Story of Paul's Rescue at Sea*

Holiday Stories

Selected stories from the New Testament to help you celebrate the Christian year

Jesus Is Born! *The Story of Christmas*

Good News! *The Story of the Shepherds*

An Amazing Star! *The Story of the Wise Men*

Hosanna! *The Story of Palm Sunday*

The Best Day Ever! *The Story of Easter*

Goodbye—for Now *The Story of Jesus' Return to Heaven*

These fifty-two books are the heart of *God Loves Me*, a Bible story program designed for young children. Individual books (or the entire set) and the accompanying program guide *God Loves Me* are available from CRC Publications (1-800-333-8300).